My Ball

Bring back my ball

I am so mad

Breathe...

It's OK to feel angry

Leave me alone

I want my ball back

Breathe...

It’s OK for me to feel this way

I can feel
better
when
I'm
ready

Is it really such a big deal?

I think I'm making too much of this

I will take my time to relax and breathe

There are lots of
other things
I like to do

I've worried too much

I'd like to feel better

Wouldn't it be nice to find something I like to do

I like feeling better

What if nothing
is wrong and
everything is alright

I can make my life better

Nothing holds me back except my own thoughts

I like
to
think
of
better
things

I like the idea
of feeling good

My Ball!